MORAL PRINCIPLES
IN EDUCATION

BY

JOHN DEWEY

SOUTHERN ILLINOIS UNIVERSITY PRESS

CARBONDALE AND EDWARDSVILLE

FEFFER & SIMONS, INC.

LONDON AND AMSTERDAM

Library of Congress Cataloging in Publication Data
Dewey, John, 1859–1952.
    Moral principles in education.
    (Arcturus books AB128)
    Reprint of the ed. published by Houghton Mifflin,
Boston, in series: Riverside educational monographs; with
new pref.
    I. Moral education. II. Title. II. Series:
Riverside educational monographs.
LC268.D4 1975   370.11´4   74-18472
ISBN 0-8093-0715-4

Arcturus Books Edition February 1975

This edition printed by offset lithography in the United
    States of America

06 05 04   13 12 11

CONTENTS

PREFACE

BY SIDNEY HOOK

JOHN DEWEY'S *Moral Principles in Education* was not the first nor the last of his discussions of moral education in school and society. It is a topic of perennial importance. Every time a political or moral crisis engulfs the nation, sooner or later the ethical deficiencies of public life are related to the prevailing ethics of the community and to the education its citizens have received, or have failed to receive, in school and out. Wherever schools have existed they have been expected to reinforce, supplement, sometimes even to substitute for, the moral education children have acquired at home or church.

Perhaps the most hoary of all prejudices about moral education is the belief that it can be taught as a separate subject-matter unrelated to all other subjects in the curriculum, that didactic instruction, whether by preaching or by less explicit means, can instill patterns of acceptable moral behavior in those subjected to this educational regimen. We smile at the notion that instruction or courses can be given in elementary virtue, intermediate virtue, or advanced virtue. But even today much of our explicit moral teaching—even when it is not sermonizing—suggests that it is a special subject encapsulated from others. I recall that in my own early school years—almost a generation after Dewey propounded his ideas about moral principles in education—a two-hour period was assigned once a week to the discussion of ethics in the rather large expectation that the behavior of the children would be improved as they made their way in the world. Alas! even the much more modest expectation that they would behave like little ladies and gentlemen when the teacher's back was turned or when she was absent from the room or school was often cruelly disappointed.

The first important point that Dewey makes is that moral principles are not separate from the social life of human beings wherever they associate; that the school is a form of social life, not a prepara-

PREFACE

tion for one; and that although the moral dimensions or aspects of the children's experience may be *distinguished* from what they learn and how they learn, they cannot be *separated* from it. To the extent that moral attitudes are acquired in school, they are acquired in the course of learning different subject-matters and through acquaintance with the different methods of achieving mastery in dealing with things and ideas.

Dewey's approach therefore undermines the conception of morality as something brought in from outside the experience of the child, as merely a command from some adult authority reinforced by fear or bribes. What is true for adults is also true, within the limits of their growth and understanding, of children. "The moral life is lived only as the individual appreciates for himself the ends for which he is working and does his work in a personal spirit of interest and devotion to these ends."

How then does the child acquire this moral sense so that it becomes effectively expressed in conduct? By instruction in all subjects that elicits an active response in testing or carrying out ideas, by learning as a form of disciplined or controlled doing

PREFACE

rather than by passive absorption of what he hears. Instead of being merely told, he is encouraged to find out by and for himself and often with others. In this way mechanical imitation is avoided, good intentions are checked by practice, and prevented from running out into reverie and daydreams. When this is properly done under the watchful supervision of good teachers, certain habits of execution are established. These habits—"reliable means of action," Dewey calls them—develop within the child perseverance, conscientiousness, fidelity, neatness, precision, concentration, cooperation, and team spirit, and other desirable traits required in carrying out his projects.

We may summarize Dewey's view by saying that the moral principles of education are to be developed through acceptance of the *morality of the task*.

It is at this point that some doubts arise. Granted that we can develop allegiance to a set of values derived from the morality of the task, are these sufficient for recognizing and accepting the values implied by the *task of morality?* Morality is not a matter of mere behavior; it is a matter of feeling, too. Character is defined not only by the traits derived from mastering a task or problem but by qualities that reveal attentiveness to and consideration for the feelings, needs, and rights of other persons. Character has an internal landscape, so to speak, reflected in the desire to be fair to others, in a complex of actions that show kindness, tact, service to the community, sometimes to the point of sacrifice. This is what many people understand as the province and task of moral education.

How, then, does Dewey achieve the transition from what we have called the morality of the task to the task of morality? His answer—original for his time and still largely disregarded—is to teach *all* subjects in such a way as to bring out and make focal their social and personal aspects, stressing how human beings are affected by them, pointing up the responsibilities that flow from their inter-relatedness. In the teaching of geography, "the ultimate significance of lake, river, mountain, and plain is not physical but social; it is the part which it plays in modifying and directing human relationships." In the teaching of history, "past events are made the means of understanding the present."

PREFACE

Even the illustrations and examples in mathematics can be related to problems suggested by the students' own experiences. Information acquired as such is not enough, especially if acquired outside the context of inquiry. It is inert; and by itself can never develop the power of judgment.

For Dewey to judge is to value. It is knowledge put to use or applied. It is not only directed to the achievement of ends but a judgment of their relative worth, their interconnection, their costs. "Judgment," says Dewey in an earlier version of this essay, "as the sense of relative values, involves ability to select, to discriminate, by reference to a standard" ("Ethical Principles underlying Education," *The Early Works of John Dewey*, 5:8). Where do we get the standard? It depends, of course, on the field in which we are judging. But where human beings are associated in "a democratic and progressive society," the standard is twofold— the degree of shared interests, and the freedom to develop new interests, both common and personal.

This involves the development of informed attitudes and dispositions that are responsive to others, susceptible to their feelings and needs.

PREFACE

Dewey is quite explicit about this. "Just as the material of objects of knowledge is related to the senses, so the material of ethical knowledge is related to emotional responsiveness." Note that Dewey uses the expression "ethical knowledge." The responsiveness must not be merely emotional. Our empathetic identifications with, and imaginative projections into, the lives of others must be based on what we know of the ways in which they can be helped or hurt, on how they really react to our outreaching efforts and overtures. Otherwise we risk falling into sentimentalism.

But what if there is no answering personal responsiveness from the others? How can moral instruction proceed if feelings are absent or dead? Dewey would reply that a child would be retarded or abnormal if he were incapable of learning about, and responding to, the purposes and ends of others. Feeling precedes and accompanies thinking in the child's interaction with his world. For in the normal course of his growth, that is how he distinguishes between things and living things, and among the latter between animals and persons. But even though the child has the natural capacity of responding to others, unless he is properly taught he may end up by treating persons as animals and animals as things. What Dewey is saying sounds paradoxical because the great tradition has separated ethical knowledge from all other knowledge, and interpreted moral principles as something "transcendental." But for Dewey what we learn and how we learn in a social context have a bearing upon subsequent conduct in all our relations with our fellows. Without destroying the spontaneity of impulse of the child, intelligent instruction can channel it into constructive activities of cooperation with others. This does not mean that we scant or neglect subject-matter and abandon intellectual discipline but that they are oriented toward the child's needs and interests in such a way that they do not appear to be a bitter medicine. Learning cannot be fun but it can be interesting and therefore enjoyable.

One can raise a more formidable challenge to Dewey's account of the nature of moral education. Character consists in activity in behalf of intelligently conceived goals that we approve after reflection. Integral to it is an element that we call

PREFACE

moral courage. The moral person or individual, according to Dewey himself, "must have the power to stand up and count for something in the actual conflicts of life." This element is embraced in the connotation of the expression "force of character." An individual who says one thing and believes another, and vice versa, or who, for example, privately disapproves of measures that debase the quality of educational experience by pandering to student transient demands but publicly supports them out of fear of the consequences of refusal, lacks "force of character."

. Granted that there is no character without intelligence. Granted that without capacity for sympathy, empathy, tact, there is no moral character. Still how account for the intelligent man who possesses the requisite sensibilities but who lacks moral courage or force of character, who is fearful of standing up to danger and the threats of danger from the mob or the crowd or a tyrant? Even when we acknowledge that the sphere of morality is coextensive with the sphere of life, this does not carry with it the requisite courage to act on the moral insight. Recognizing that human beings differ in their native endowment with respect to their response to danger and pain and uncertainty, Dewey would probably rely on education to strengthen the propensies to stake what we have, what we are, and what we think, in our commitment to the right when conflicts arise. Education must also develop the willingness to take risks in behalf of our moral vision, otherwise we betray ourselves and others, too.

But how? He does not say. Can it be done by providing models of behavior, finding and celebrating them in history, art, and literature? Can situations be organized in which individuals can test themselves and learn both from their failures and their unwillingness to risk failure? We still do not know. But Dewey's approach does provide us with insights and principles that undoubtedly will enter into any proposed method of overcoming the gap between the well-intentioned commitment to intelligent policies, and their courageous and effective execution. If knowledge is to make a difference in creating a better world or resisting those forces and individuals whose actions would result in a worse world, education must find the ways.

THE MORAL PURPOSE OF
THE SCHOOL

I

THE MORAL PURPOSE OF
THE SCHOOL

An English contemporary philosopher has called
attention to the difference between moral ideas
and ideas about morality. " Moral ideas " are ideas
of any sort whatsoever which take effect in conduct and improve it, make it better than it otherwise would be. Similarly, one may say, immoral
ideas are ideas of whatever sort (whether arith-
metical or geographical or physiological) which
show themselves in making behavior worse than
it would otherwise be; and non-moral ideas, one
may say, are such ideas and pieces of information as leave conduct uninfluenced for either the
better or the worse. Now "ideas about morality "
may be morally indifferent or immoral or moral.
There is nothing in the nature of ideas *about*
morality, of information *about* honesty or purity
or kindness which automatically transmutes such
ideas into good character or good conduct.

MORAL PRINCIPLES

This distinction between moral ideas, ideas of any sort whatsoever that have become a part of character and hence a part of the working motives of behavior, and ideas *about* moral action that may remain as inert and ineffective as if they were so much knowledge about Egyptian archæology, is fundamental to the discussion of moral education. The business of the educator — whether parent or teacher — is to see to it that the greatest possible number of ideas acquired by children and youth are acquired in such a vital way that they become *moving* ideas, motive-forces in the guidance of conduct. This demand and this opportunity make the moral purpose universal and dominant in all instruction — whatsoever the topic. Were it not for this possibility, the familiar statement that the ultimate purpose of all education is character-forming would be hypocritical pretense; for as every one knows, the direct and immediate attention of teachers and pupils must be, for the greater part of the time, upon intellectual matters. It is out of the question to keep direct moral considerations constantly uppermost. But it is not out of the question to aim at making the methods of learning, of acquiring intellectual power, and of assimilating subject-matter, such that they will render behavior more enlightened, more consistent, more vigorous than it otherwise would be.

The same distinction between "moral ideas" and "ideas about morality" explains for us a source of continual misunderstanding between teachers in the schools and critics of education outside of the schools. The latter look through the school programmes, the school courses of study, and do not find any place set apart for instruction in ethics or for "moral teaching." Then they assert that the schools are doing nothing, or next to nothing, for character-training; they become emphatic, even vehement, about the moral deficiencies of public education. The school-teachers, on the other hand, resent these criticisms as an injustice, and hold not only that they do "teach morals," but that they teach them every moment of the day, five days in the week. In this contention the teachers *in principle* are in the right; if they are in the wrong, it is not because special periods are not set aside for what

3

after all can only be teaching *about* morals, but because their own characters, or their school atmosphere and ideals, or their methods of teaching, or the subject-matter which they teach, are not such *in detail* as to bring intellectual results into vital union with character so that they become working forces in behavior. Without discussing, therefore, the limits or the value of so-called direct moral instruction (or, better, instruction *about* morals), it may be laid down as fundamental that the influence of direct moral instruction, even at its very best, is *comparatively* small in amount and slight in influence, when the whole field of moral growth through education is taken into account. This larger field of indirect and vital moral education, the development of character through all the agencies, instrumentalities, and materials of school life is, therefore, the subject of our present discussion.

THE MORAL TRAINING GIVEN
BY THE SCHOOL COMMUNITY

THE MORAL TRAINING GIVEN BY THE SCHOOL COMMUNITY

THERE cannot be two sets of ethical principles, one for life in the school, and the other for life outside of the school. As conduct is one, so also the principles of conduct are one. The tendency to discuss the morals of the school as if the school were an institution by itself is highly unfortunate. The moral responsibility of the school, and of those who conduct it, is to society. The school is fundamentally an institution erected by society to do a certain specific work, — to exercise a certain specific function in maintaining the life and advancing the welfare of society. The educational system which does not recognize that this fact entails upon it an ethical responsibility is derelict and a defaulter. It is not doing what it was called into existence to do, and what it pretends to do. Hence the entire structure of the school in general and its concrete workings in particular need to be considered from time to time with reference to the social position and function of the school.

The idea that the moral work and worth of the public school system as a whole are to be measured by its social value is, indeed, a familiar notion. However, it is frequently taken in too limited and rigid a way. The social work of the school is often limited to training for citizenship, and citizenship is then interpreted in a narrow sense as meaning capacity to vote intelligently, disposition to obey laws, etc. But it is futile to contract and cramp the ethical responsibility of the school in this way. The child is one, and he must either live his social life as an integral unified being, or suffer loss and create friction. To pick out one of the many social relations which the child bears, and to define the work of the school by that alone, is like instituting a vast and complicated system of physical exercise which would have for its object simply the development of the lungs and the power of breathing, independent of other organs and functions. The child is an organic whole, intellectually, socially, and morally, as well as physically. We must take the child as a member of society in the broadest sense, and demand for and from the schools whatever is necessary to enable the child intelligently to recognize all his social relations and take his part in sustaining them.

To isolate the formal relationship of citizenship from the whole system of relations with which it is actually interwoven ; to suppose that there is some one particular study or mode of treatment which can make the child a good citizen ; to suppose, in other words, that a good citizen is anything more than a thoroughly efficient and serviceable member of society, one with all his powers of body and mind under control, is a hampering superstition which it is hoped may soon disappear from educational discussion.

The child is to be not only a voter and a subject of law ; he is also to be a member of a family, himself in turn responsible, in all probability, for rearing and training of future children, thereby maintaining the continuity of society. He is to be a worker, engaged in some occupation which will be of use to society, and which will maintain his own independence and self-respect. He is to be a member of some particular neighborhood and community, and must contribute to the values of life, add to the decencies and graces of civilization wherever he is. These are bare and formal statements, but if we let our imagination translate them into their concrete details, we have a wide and varied scene. For the child properly to take his place in reference to these various functions means training in science, in art, in history ; means command of the fundamental methods of inquiry and the fundamental tools of intercourse and communication ; means a trained and sound body, skillful eye and hand ; means habits of industry, perseverance ; in short, habits of serviceableness.

Moreover, the society of which the child is to be a member is, in the United States, a democratic and progressive society. The child must be educated for leadership as well as for obedience. He must have power of self-direction and power of directing others, power of administration, ability to assume positions of responsibility. This necessity of educating for leadership is as great on the industrial as on the political side.

New inventions, new machines, new methods of

transportation and intercourse are making over the whole scene of action year by year. It is an absolute impossibility to educate the child for any fixed station in life. So far as education is conducted unconsciously or consciously on this basis, it results in fitting the future citizen for no station in life, but makes him a drone, a hanger-on, or an actual retarding influence in the onward movement. Instead of caring for himself and for others, he becomes one who has himself to be cared for. Here, too, the ethical responsibility of the school on the social side must be interpreted in the broadest and freest spirit ; it is equivalent to that training of the child which will give him such possession of himself that he may take charge of himself ; may not only adapt himself to the changes that are going on, but have power to shape and direct them.

Apart from participation in social life, the school has no moral end nor aim. As long as we confine ourselves to the school as an isolated institution, we have no directing principles, because we have no object. For example, the end of education is said to be the harmonious development of all the powers of the individual. Here no reference to social life or membership is apparent, and yet many think we have in it an adequate and thoroughgoing definition of the goal of education. But if this definition be taken independently of social relationship we have no way of telling what is meant by any one of the terms employed. We do not know what a power is; we do not know what development is; we do not know what harmony is. A power is a power only with reference to the use to which it is put, the function it has to serve. If we leave out the uses supplied by social life we have nothing but the old "faculty psychology" to tell what is meant by power and what the specific powers are. The principle reduces itself to enumerating a lot of faculties like perception, memory, reasoning, etc., and then stating that each one of these powers needs to be developed.

Education then becomes a gymnastic exercise. Acute powers of observation and memory might be developed by studying Chinese characters; acuteness in reasoning might be got by discussing the scholastic subtleties of the Middle

Ages. The simple fact is that there is no isolated faculty of observation, or memory, or reasoning anymore than there is an original faculty of black-smithing, carpentering, or steam engineering. Faculties mean simply that particular impulses and habits have been coördinated or framed with reference to accomplishing certain definite kinds of work. We need to know the social situations in which the individual will have to use ability to observe, recollect, imagine, and reason, in order to have any way of telling what a training of men-tal powers actually means.

What holds in the illustration of this particu-lar definition of education holds good from what-ever point of view we approach the matter. Only as we interpret school activities with reference to the larger circle of social activities to which they relate do we find any standard for judging their moral significance.

The school itself must be a vital social insti-tution to a much greater extent than obtains at present. I am told that there is a swimming school in a certain city where youth are taught to swim without going into the water, being repeatedly drilled in the various movements which are necessary for swimming. When one of the young men so trained was asked what he did when he got into the water, he laconically replied, "Sunk." The story happens to be true; were it not, it would seem to be a fable made expressly for the purpose of typifying the ethical relationship of school to society. The school cannot be a preparation for social life excepting as it reproduces, within itself, typical conditions of social life. At present it is largely engaged in the futile task of Sisyphus. It is endeavoring to form habits in children for use in a social life which, it would almost seem, is carefully and purposely kept away from vital contact with the child undergoing training. The only way to prepare for social life is to engage in social life. To form habits of social usefulness and serviceableness apart from any direct social need and motive, apart from any existing social situation, is, to the letter, teaching the child to swim by going through motions outside of the water. The most indispensable condition is left out of account, and the results are correspondingly partial.

IN EDUCATION

The much lamented separation in the schools of intellectual and moral training, of acquiring information and growing in character, is simply one expression of the failure to conceive and construct the school as a social institution, having social life and value within itself. Except so far as the school is an embryonic typical community life, moral training must be partly pathological and partly formal. Training is pathological when stress is laid upon correcting wrong-doing instead of upon forming habits of positive service. Too often the teacher's concern with the moral life of pupils takes the form of alertness for failures to conform to school rules and routine. These regulations, judged from the standpoint of the development of the child at the time, are more or less conventional and arbitrary. They are rules which have to be made in order that the existing modes of school work may go on ; but the lack of inherent necessity in these school modes reflects itself in a feeling, on the part of the child, that the moral discipline of the school is arbitrary. Any conditions that compel the teacher to take note of failures rather than of healthy growth

15

give false standards and result in distortion and perversion. Attending to wrong-doing ought to be an incident rather than a principle. The child ought to have a positive consciousness of what he is about, so as to judge his acts from the standpoint of reference to the work which he has to do. Only in this way does he have a vital standard, one that enables him to turn failures to account for the future.

By saying that the moral training of the school is formal, I mean that the moral habits currently emphasized by the school are habits which are created, as it were, *ad hoc*. Even the habits of promptness, regularity, industry, non-interference with the work of others, faithfulness to tasks imposed, which are specially inculcated in the school, are habits that are necessary simply because the school system is what it is, and must be preserved intact. If we grant the inviolability of the school system as it is, these habits represent permanent and necessary moral ideas; but just in so far as the school system is itself isolated and mechanical, insistence upon these moral habits is more or less unreal, because the ideal to which they relate is not itself necessary. The duties, in other words, are distinctly school duties, not life duties. If we compare this condition with that of the well-ordered home, we find that the duties and responsibilities that the child has there to recognize do not belong to the family as a specialized and isolated institution, but flow from the very nature of the social life in which the family participates and to which it contributes. The child ought to have the same motives for right doing and to be judged by the same standards in the school, as the adult in the wider social life to which he belongs. Interest in community welfare, an interest that is intellectual and practical, as well as emotional — an interest, that is to say, in perceiving whatever makes for social order and progress, and in carrying these principles into execution — is the moral habit to which all the special school habits must be related if they are to be animated by the breath of life.

THE MORAL TRAINING FROM
METHODS OF INSTRUCTION

III

THE MORAL TRAINING FROM METHODS OF INSTRUCTION

THE principle of the social character of the school as the basic factor in the moral education given may be also applied to the question of methods of instruction, — not in their details, but their general spirit. The emphasis then falls upon construction and giving out, rather than upon absorption and mere learning. We fail to recognize how essentially individualistic the latter methods are, and how unconsciously, yet certainly and effectively, they react into the child's ways of judging and of acting. Imagine forty children all engaged in reading the same books, and in preparing and reciting the same lessons day after day. Suppose this process constitutes by far the larger part of their work, and that they are continually judged from the standpoint of what they are able to take in in a study hour and reproduce in a recitation hour. There is next to no opportunity for any social division of labor. There is no opportunity for each child to work out something specifically his own, which he may contribute to the common stock, while he, in turn, participates in the productions of others. All are set to do exactly the same work and turn out the same products. The social spirit is not cultivated, —in fact, in so far as the purely individualistic method gets in its work, it atrophies for lack of use. One reason why reading aloud in school is. poor is that the real motive for the use of language—the desire to communicate and to learn —is not utilized. The child knows perfectly well that the teacher and all his fellow pupils have exactly the same facts and ideas before them that he has ; he is not *giving* them anything at all. And it may be questioned whether the moral lack is not as great as the intellectual. The child is born with a natural desire to give out, to do, to serve. When this tendency is not used, when conditions are such that other motives are substituted, the accumulation of an influence working against the social spirit is much larger than we have any idea of, —especially when the burden of work, week after week, and year after year, falls upon this side.

But lack of cultivation of the social spirit is not all. Positively individualistic motives and standards are inculcated. Some stimulus must be found to keep the child at his studies. At the best this will be his affection for his teacher, together with a feeling that he is not violating school rules, and thus negatively, if not positively, is contributing to the good of the school. I have nothing to say against these motives so far as they go, but they are inadequate. The relation between the piece of work to be done and affection for a third person is external, not intrinsic. It is therefore liable to break down whenever the external conditions are changed. Moreover, this attachment to a particular person, while in a way social, may become so isolated· and exclusive as to be selfish in quality. In any case, the child should gradually grow out of this relatively external motive into an appreciation, for its own sake, of the social value of what he has to do, because of its larger relations to life, not pinned down to two or three persons.

MORAL PRINCIPLES

But, unfortunately, the motive is not always at this relative best, but mixed with lower motives which are distinctly egoistic. Fear is a motive which is almost sure to enter in,—not necessarily physical fear, or fear of punishment, but fear of losing the approbation of others; or fear of failure, so extreme as to be morbid and paralyzing. On the other side, emulation and rivalry enter in. Just because all are doing the same work, and are judged (either in recitation or examination with reference to grading and to promotion) not from the standpoint of their personal contribution, but from that of *comparative* success, the feeling of superiority over others is unduly appealed to, while timid children are depressed. Children are judged with reference to their capacity to realize the same external standard. The weaker gradually lose their sense of power, and accept a position of continuous and persistent inferiority. The effect upon both self-respect and respect for work need not be dwelt upon. The strong learn to glory, not in their strength, but in the fact that they are stronger. The child is prematurely launched into the region of individualistic competition, and this in a direction where competition is least applicable, namely, in intellectual and artistic matters, whose law is co-operation and participation.

Next, perhaps, to the evils of passive absorption and of competition for external standing come, perhaps, those which result from the eternal emphasis upon preparation for a remote future. I do not refer here to the waste of energy and vitality that accrues when children, who live so largely in the immediate present, are appealed to in the name of a dim and uncertain future which means little or nothing to them. I have in mind rather the habitual procrastination that develops when the motive for work is future, not present; and the false standards of judgment that are created when work is estimated, not on the basis of present need and present responsibility, but by reference to an external result, like passing an examination, getting promoted, entering high school, getting into college, etc. Who can reckon up the loss of moral power that arises from the constant impression that nothing is worth doing in itself, but only as a preparation for something else, which in turn is only a getting ready for some genuinely serious end beyond? Moreover, as a rule, it will be found that remote success is an end which appeals most to those in whom egoistic desire to get ahead — to get ahead of others — is already only too strong a motive. Those in whom personal ambition is already so strong that it paints glowing pictures of future victories may be touched ; others of a more generous nature do not respond.

I cannot stop to paint the other side. I can only say that the introduction of every method that appeals to the child's active powers, to his capacities in construction, production, and creation, marks an opportunity to shift the centre of ethical gravity from an absorption which is selfish to a service which is social. Manual training is more than manual ; it is more than intellectual ; in the hands of any good teacher it lends itself easily, and almost as a matter of course, to development of social habits. Ever since the philosophy of Kant, it has been a commonplace of æsthetic theory, that art is universal ; that it is not the product of purely personal desire or appetite, or capable of merely individual appropriation, but has a value participated in by all who perceive it. Even in the schools where most conscious attention is paid to moral considerations, the methods of study and recitation may be such as to emphasize appreciation rather than power, an emotional readiness to assimilate the experiences of others, rather than enlightened and trained capacity to carry forward those values which in other conditions and past times made those experiences worth having. At all events, separation between instruction and character continues in our schools (in spite of the efforts of individual teachers) as a result of divorce between learning and doing. The attempt to attach genuine moral effectiveness to the mere processes of learning, and to the habits which go along with learning, can result only in a training infected with formality, arbitrariness, and an undue emphasis upon failure to conform. That there is as much accomplished as there is shows the possibilities involved in methods of school activity which afford opportunity for reciprocity, coöperation, and positive personal achievement.

THE SOCIAL NATURE OF THE
COURSE OF STUDY

IV

THE SOCIAL NATURE OF THE COURSE OF STUDY

In many respects, it is the subject-matter used in school life which decides both the general atmosphere of the school and the methods of instruction and discipline which rule. A barren "course of study," that is to say, a meagre and narrow field of school activities, cannot possibly lend itself to the development of a vital social spirit or to methods that appeal to sympathy and coöperation instead of to absorption, exclusiveness, and competition. Hence it becomes an all important matter to know how we shall apply our social standard of moral value to the subject-matter of school work, to what we call, traditionally, the "studies" that occupy pupils.

A study is to be considered as a means of bringing the child to realize the social scene of action. Thus considered it gives a criterion for selection of material and for judgment of values. We have at present three independent values set up: one of culture, another of information, and another of discipline. In reality, these refer only to three phases of social interpretation. Information is genuine or educative only in so far as it presents definite images and conceptions of materials placed in a context of social life. Discipline is genuinely educative only as it represents a reaction of information into the individual's own powers so that he brings them under control for social ends. Culture, if it is to be genuinely educative and not an external polish or factitious varnish, represents the vital union of information and discipline. It marks the socialization of the individual in his outlook upon life.

This point may be illustrated by brief reference to a few of the school studies. In the first place, there is no line of demarkation within facts themselves which classifies them as belonging to science, history, or geography, respectively. The pigeon-hole classification which is so prevalent at present (fostered by introducing the pupil at the outset into a number of different studies contained in different text-books) gives an utterly erroneous idea of the relations of studies to one another and to the intellectual whole to which all belong. In fact, these subjects have to do with the same ultimate reality, namely, the conscious experience of man. It is only because we have different interests, or different ends, that we sort out the material and label part of it science, part of it history, part geography, and so on. Each "sorting" represents materials arranged with reference to some one dominant typical aim or process of the social life.

This social criterion is necessary, not only to mark off studies from one another, but also to grasp the reasons for each study, — the motives in connection with which it shall be presented. How, for example, should we define geography? What is the unity in the different so-called divisions of geography, — mathematical geography, physical geography, political geography, commercial geography? Are they purely empirical classifications dependent upon the brute fact that we run across a lot of different facts? Or is there some intrinsic principle through which the material is distributed under these various heads, — something in the interest and attitude of the human mind towards them? I should say that geography has to do with all those aspects of social life which are concerned with the interaction of the life of man and nature; or, that it has to do with the world considered as the scene of social interaction. Any fact, then, will be geographical in so far as it has to do with the dependence of man upon his natural environment, or with changes introduced in this environment through the life of man.

The four forms of geography referred to above represent, then, four increasing stages of abstraction in discussing the mutual relation of human life and nature. The beginning must be social geography, the frank recognition of the earth as the home of men acting in relations to one another. I mean by this that the essence of any geographical fact is the consciousness of two persons, or two groups of persons, who are at once separated and connected by their physical environment, and that the interest is in seeing how these people are at once kept apart and brought together in their actions by the instrumentality of the physical environment.

IN EDUCATION

The ultimate significance of lake, river, mountain, and plain is not physical but social; it is the part which it plays in modifying and directing human relationships. This evidently involves an extension of the term commercial. It has to do not simply with business, in the narrow sense, but with whatever relates to human intercourse and intercommunication as affected by natural forms and properties. Political geography represents this same social interaction taken in a static instead of in a dynamic way; taken, that is, as temporarily crystallized and fixed in certain forms. Physical geography (including under this not simply physiography, but also the study of flora and fauna) represents a further analysis or abstraction. It studies the conditions which determine human action, leaving out of account, temporarily, the ways in which they concretely do this. Mathematical geography carries the analysis back to more ultimate and remote conditions, showing that the physical conditions of the earth are not ultimate, but depend upon the place which the world occupies in a larger system. Here, in other words, are traced, step by step, the links

35

which connect the immediate social occupations and groupings of men with the whole natural system which ultimately conditions them. Step by step the scene is enlarged and the image of what enters into the make-up of social action is widened and broadened ; at no time is the chain of connection to be broken.

It is out of the question to take up the studies one by one and show that their meaning is similarly controlled by social considerations. But I cannot forbear saying a word or two upon history. History is vital or dead to the child according as it is, or is not, presented from the sociological standpoint. When treated simply as a record of what has passed and gone, it must be mechanical, because the past, as the past, is remote. Simply as the past there is no motive for attending to it. The ethical value of history teaching will be measured by the extent to which past events are made the means of understanding the present,— affording insight into what makes up the structure and working of society to-day. Existing social structure is exceedingly complex. It is practically impossible for the child to attack it *en masse* and get any definite mental image of it. But type phases of historical development may be selected which will exhibit, as through a telescope, the essential constituents of the existing order. Greece, for example, represents what art and growing power of individual expression stand for; Rome exhibits the elements and forces of political life on a tremendous scale. Or, as these civilizations are themselves relatively complex, a study of still simpler forms of hunting, nomadic, and agricultural life in the beginnings of civilization, a study of the effects of the introduction of iron, and iron tools, reduces the complexity to simpler elements.

One reason historical teaching is usually not more effective is that the student is set to acquire information in such a way that no epochs or factors stand out in his mind as typical; everything is reduced to the same dead level. The way to secure the necessary perspective is to treat the past as if it were a projected present with some of its elements enlarged.

The principle of contrast is as important as that of similarity. Because the present life is so close to us, touching us at every point, we cannot get away from it to see it as it really is. Nothing stands out clearly or sharply as characteristic. In the study of past periods, attention necessarily attaches itself to striking differences. Thus the child gets a locus of imagination, through which he can remove himself from the pressure of present surrounding circumstances and define them.

History is equally available in teaching the *methods* of social progress. It is commonly stated that history must be studied from the standpoint of cause and effect. The truth of this statement depends upon its interpretation. Social life is so complex and the various parts of it are so organically related to one another and to the natural environment, that it is impossible to say that this or that thing is the cause of some other particular thing. But the study of history can reveal the main instruments in the discoveries, inventions, new modes of life, etc., which have initiated the great epochs of social advance; and it can present to the child types of the main lines of social progress, and can set before him what have been the chief difficulties and obstructions in the way of progress. Once more this can be done only in so far as it is recognized that social forces in themselves are always the same, —that the same kind of influences were at work one hundred and one thousand years ago that are now working, — and that particular historical epochs afford illustration of the way in which the fundamental forces work.

Everything depends, then, upon history being treated from a social standpoint; as manifesting the agencies which have influenced social development and as presenting the typical institutions in which social life has expressed itself. The culture-epoch theory, while working in the right direction, has failed to recognize the importance of treating past periods with relation to the present, — as affording insight into the representative factors of its structure; it has treated these periods too much as if they had some meaning or value in themselves. The way in which the biographical method is handled illustrates the same point. It is often treated in such a way as to exclude from the child's consciousness (or at least not sufficiently to emphasize) the social

39

forces and principles involved in the association of the masses of men. It is quite true that the child is easily interested in history from the biographical standpoint; but unless "the hero" is treated in relation to the community life behind him that he sums up and directs, there is danger that history will reduce itself to a mere exciting story. Then moral instruction reduces itself to drawing certain lessons from the life of the particular personalities concerned, instead of widening and deepening the child's imagination of social relations, ideals, and means.

It will be remembered that I am not making these points for their own sake, but with reference to the general principle that when a study is taught as a mode of understanding social life it has positive ethical import. What the normal child continuously needs is not so much isolated moral lessons upon the importance of truthfulness and honesty, or the beneficent results that follow from a particular act of patriotism, as the formation of habits of social imagination and conception.

I take one more illustration, namely, mathematics. This does, or does not, accomplish its full purpose according as it is, or is not, presented as a social tool. The prevailing divorce between information and character, between knowledge and social action, stalks upon the scene here. The moment mathematical study is severed from the place which it occupies with reference to use in social life, it becomes unduly abstract, even upon the purely intellectual side. It is presented as a matter of technical relations and formulæ apart from any end or use. What the study of number suffers from in elementary education is lack of motivation. Back of this and that and the other particular bad method is the radical mistake of treating number as if it were an end in itself, instead of the means of accomplishing some end. Let the child get a consciousness of what is the use of number, of what it really is for, and half the battle is won. Now this consciousness of the use of reason implies some end which is implicitly social.

One of the absurd things in the more advanced study of arithmetic is the extent to which the child is introduced to numerical operations which have no distinctive mathematical principles characterizing them, but which represent certain general principles found in business relationships. To train the child in these operations, while paying no attention to the business realities in which they are of use, or to the conditions of social life which make these business activities necessary, is neither arithmetic nor common sense. The child is called upon to do examples in interest, partnership, banking, brokerage, and so on through a long string, and no pains are taken to see that, in connection with the arithmetic, he has any sense of the social realities involved. This part of arithmetic is essentially sociological in its nature. It ought either to be omitted entirely, or else be taught in connection with a study of the relevant social realities. As we now manage the study, it is the old case of learning to swim apart from the water over again, with correspondingly bad results on the practical side.

In concluding this portion of the discussion, we may say that our conceptions of moral education have been too narrow, too formal, and too pathological. We have associated the term ethical with certain special acts which are labeled virtues and are set off from the mass of other acts, and are still more divorced from the habitual images and motives of the children performing them. Moral instruction is thus associated with teaching about these particular virtues, or with instilling certain sentiments in regard to them. The moral has been conceived in too goody-goody a way. Ultimate moral motives and forces are nothing more or less than social intelligence — the power of observing and comprehending social situations, — and social power — trained capacities of control — at work in the service of social interest and aims. There is no fact which throws light upon the constitution of society, there is no power whose training adds to social resourcefulness that is not moral.

I sum up, then, this part of the discussion by asking your attention to the moral trinity of the school. The demand is for social intelligence, social power, and social interests. Our resources are (1) the life of the school as a social institution in itself; (2) methods of learning and of doing work ; and (3) the school studies or curriculum. In so far as the school represents, in its own spirit, a genuine community life; in so far as what are called school discipline, government, order, etc., are the expressions of this inherent social spirit; in so far as the methods used are those that appeal to the active and constructive powers, permitting the child to give out and thus to serve; in so far as the curriculum is so selected and organized as to provide the material for affording the child a consciousness of the world in which he has to play a part, and the demands he has to meet; so far as these ends are met, the school is organized on an ethical basis. So far as general principles are concerned, all the basic ethical requirements are met. The rest remains between the individual teacher and the individual child.

THE PSYCHOLOGICAL ASPECT
OF MORAL EDUCATION

V

THE PSYCHOLOGICAL ASPECT
OF MORAL EDUCATION

So far we have been considering the make-up of purposes and results that constitute conduct — its " what." But conduct has a certain method and spirit also — its "how." Conduct may be looked upon as expressing the attitudes and dispositions of an *individual*, as well as realizing social results and maintaining the social fabric. A consideration of conduct as a mode of individual performance, personal doing, takes us from the social to the psychological side of morals. In the first place, all conduct springs ultimately and radically out of native instincts and impulses. We must know what these instincts and impulses are, and what they are at each particular stage of the child's development, in order to know what to appeal to and what to build upon. Neglect of this principle may give a mechanical imitation of moral conduct, but the imitation will be ethically dead, because it is external and has its centre without, not within, the individual. We must study the child, in other words, to get our indications, our symptoms, our suggestions. The more or less spontaneous acts of the child are not to be thought of as setting moral forms to which the efforts of the educator must conform—this would result simply in spoiling the child; but they are symptoms which require to be interpreted: stimuli which need to be responded to in directed ways; material which, in however transformed a shape, is the only ultimate constituent of future moral conduct and character.

Then, secondly, our ethical principles need to be stated in psychological terms because the child supplies us with the only means or instruments by which to realize moral ideals. The subject-matter of the curriculum, however important, however judiciously selected, is empty of conclusive moral content until it is made over into terms of the individual's own activities, habits, and desires. We must know what history, geography, and mathematics mean in psychological terms, that is, as modes of personal experiencing, before

48

we can get out of them their moral potentialities.

The psychological side of education sums itself up, of course, in a consideration of character. It is a commonplace to say that the development of character is the end of all school work. The difficulty lies in the execution of the idea. And an underlying difficulty in this execution is the lack of a clear conception of what character means. This may seem an extreme statement. If so, the idea may be conveyed by saying that we generally conceive of character simply in terms of results; we have no clear conception of it in psychological terms — that is, as a process, as working or dynamic. We know what character means in terms of the actions which proceed from it, but we have not a definite conception of it on its inner side, as a system of working forces.

(1) Force, efficiency in execution, or overt action, is one necessary constituent of character. In our moral books and lectures we may lay the stress upon good intentions, etc. But we know practically that the kind of character we hope to build up through our education is one that not

only has good intentions, but that insists upon carrying them out. Any other character is wishy-washy ; it is goody, not good. The individual must have the power to stand up and count for something in the actual conflicts of life. He must have initiative, insistence, persistence, courage, and industry. He must, in a word, have all that goes under the name "*force* of character." Undoubtedly, individuals differ greatly in their native endowment in this respect. None the less, each has a certain primary equipment of impulse, of tendency forward, of innate urgency to do. The problem of education on this side is that of discovering what this native fund of power is, and then of utilizing it in such a way (affording conditions which both stimulate and control) as to organize it into definite conserved modes of action — habits.

(2) But something more is required than sheer force. Sheer force may be brutal; it may override the interests of others. Even when aiming at right ends it may go at them in such a way as to violate the rights of others. More than this, in sheer force there is no guarantee for the right

end. Efficiency may be directed towards mistaken ends and result in positive mischief and destruction. Power, as already suggested, must be directed. It must be organized along social channels ; it must be attached to valuable ends.

This involves training on both the intellectual and emotional side. On the intellectual side we must have judgment — what is ordinarily called good sense. The difference between mere knowledge, or information, and judgment is that the former is simply held, not used ; judgment is knowledge directed with reference to the accomplishment of ends. Good judgment is a sense of respective or proportionate values. The one who has judgment is the one who has ability to size up a situation. He is the one who can grasp the scene or situation before him, ignoring what is irrelevant, or what for the time being is unimportant, who can seize upon the factors which demand attention, and grade them according to their respective claims. Mere knowledge of what the right is, in the abstract, mere intentions of following the right in general, however praiseworthy in themselves, are never a substitute for this power of trained judgment. Action is always in the concrete. It is definite and individualized. Except, therefore, as it is backed and controlled by a knowledge of the actual concrete factors in the situation in which it occurs, it must be relatively futile and waste.

(3) But the consciousness of ends must be more than merely intellectual. We can imagine a person with most excellent judgment, who yet does not act upon his judgment. There must not only be force to insure effort in execution against obstacles, but there must also be a delicate personal responsiveness, — there must be an emotional reaction. Indeed, good judgment is impossible without this susceptibility. Unless there is a prompt and almost instinctive sensitiveness to conditions, to the ends and interests of others, the intellectual side of judgment will not have proper material to work upon. Just as the material of knowledge is supplied through the senses, so the material of ethical knowledge is supplied by emotional responsiveness. It is difficult to put this quality into words, but we all know the difference between the character which is hard and

formal, and one which is sympathetic, flexible, and open. In the abstract the former may be as sincerely devoted to moral ideas as is the latter, but as a practical matter we prefer to live with the latter. We count upon it to accomplish more by tact, by instinctive recognition of the claims of others, by skill in adjusting, than the former can accomplish by mere attachment to rules.

Here, then, is the moral standard, by which to test the work of the school upon the side of what it does directly for individuals. (*a*) Does the school as a system, at present, attach sufficient importance to the spontaneous instincts and impulses? Does it afford sufficient opportunity for these to assert themselves and work out their own results? Can we even say that the school in principle attaches itself, at present, to the active constructive powers rather than to processes of absorption and learning? Does not our talk about self-activity largely render itself meaningless because the self-activity we have in mind is purely "intellectual," out of relation to those impulses which work through hand and eye?

53

MORAL PRINCIPLES

Just in so far as the present school methods fail to meet the test of such questions moral results must be unsatisfactory. We cannot secure the development of positive force of character unless we are willing to pay its price. We cannot smother and repress the child's powers, or gradually abort them (from failure of opportunity for exercise), and then expect a character with initiative and consecutive industry. I am aware of the importance attaching to inhibition, but mere inhibition is valueless. The only restraint, the only holding-in, that is of any worth is that which comes through holding powers concentrated upon a positive end. An end cannot be attained excepting as instincts and impulses are kept from discharging at random and from running off on side tracks. In keeping powers at work upon their relevant ends, there is sufficient opportunity for genuine inhibition. To say that inhibition is higher than power, is like saying that death is more than life, negation more than affirmation, sacrifice more than service.

(*b*) We must also test our school work by finding whether it affords the conditions necessary for the formation of good judgment. Judgment as the sense of relative values involves ability to select, to discriminate. Acquiring information can never develop the power of judgment. Development of judgment is in spite of, not because of, methods of instruction that emphasize simple learning. The test comes only when the information acquired has to be put to use. Will it do what we expect of it ? I have heard an educator of large experience say that in her judgment the greatest defect of instruction to-day, on the intellectual side, is found in the fact that children leave school without a mental perspective. Facts seem to them all of the same importance. There is no foreground or background. There is no instinctive habit of sorting out facts upon a scale of worth and of grading them.

The child cannot get power of judgment excepting as he is continually exercised in forming and testing judgments. He must have an opportunity to select for himself, and to attempt to put his selections into execution, that he may submit them to the final test, that of action. Only thus can he learn to discriminate that which promises success from that which promises failure; only thus can he form the habit of relating his purposes and notions to the conditions that determine their value. Does the school, as a system, afford at present sufficient opportunity for this sort of experimentation? Except so far as the emphasis of the school work is upon intelligent doing, upon active investigation, it does not furnish the conditions necessary for that exercise of judgment which is an integral factor in good character.

(c) I shall be brief with respect to the other point, the need of susceptibility and responsiveness. The informally social side of education, the æsthetic environment and influences, are all-important. In so far as the work is laid out in regular and formulated ways, so far as there are lacking opportunities for casual and free social intercourse between pupils and between the pupils and the teacher, this side of the child's nature is either starved, or else left to find haphazard expression along more or less secret channels. When the school system, under plea of the practical (meaning by the practical the narrowly utili-

tarian), confines the child to the three R's and
the formal studies connected with them, shuts
him out from the vital in literature and history,
and deprives him of his right to contact with
what is best in architecture, music, sculpture, and
picture, it is hopeless to expect definite results
in the training of sympathetic openness and responsiveness.

What we need in education is a genuine faith
in the existence of moral principles which are
capable of effective application. We believe, so
far as the mass of children are concerned, that if
we keep at them long enough we can teach reading and writing and figuring. We are practically,
even if unconsciously, skeptical as to the possibility of anything like the same assurance in
morals. We believe in moral laws and rules, to
be sure, but they are in the air. They are something set off by themselves. They are so *very*
"moral" that they have no working contact with
the average affairs of every-day life. These moral
principles need to be brought down to the ground
through their statement in social and in psy-

chological terms. We need to see that moral principles are not arbitrary, that they are not "transcendental"; that the term "moral" does not designate a special region or portion of life. We need to translate the moral into the conditions and forces of our community life, and into the impulses and habits of the individual.

All the rest is mint, anise, and cummin. The one thing needful is that we recognize that moral principles are real in the same sense in which other forces are real; that they are inherent in community life, and in the working structure of the individual. If we can secure a genuine faith in this fact, we shall have secured the condition which alone is necessary to get from our educational system all the effectiveness there is in it. The teacher who operates in this faith will find every subject, every method of instruction, every incident of school life pregnant with moral possibility.

OUTLINE

59

OUTLINE

OUTLINE

TEXTUAL NOTE: The text of *Moral Principles in Education* published here is a photo-offset reprint of the first printing (Boston: Houghton Mifflin Company, The Riverside Press, Cambridge, 1909). No emendations have been made in the text. The Preface by Sidney Hook substitutes for the Introduction [by Henry Suzzallo].   J. A. B.